MY GUIDE TO US CITIZENSHIP

IMMIGRATION
IN THE US

Tammy
Gagne

Mitchell Lane
PUBLISHERS
P.O. Box 196
Hockessin, DE 19707
www.mitchelllane.com

Mitchell Lane
PUBLISHERS

MY GUIDE TO
US CITIZENSHIP

Immigration in the US
US Immigration Services
US Laws of Citizenship
Your Guide to Becoming a US Citizen

Copyright © 2014 by Mitchell Lane Publishers

Printing 1 2 3 4 5 6 7 8 9

PUBLISHER'S NOTE: The facts on which this book is based have been thoroughly researched. Documentation of such research can be found on page 44. While every possible effort has been made to ensure accuracy, the publisher will not assume liability for damages caused by inaccuracies in the data, and makes no warranty on the accuracy of the information contained herein.

The Internet sites referenced herein were active as of the publication date. Due to the fleeting nature of some web sites, we cannot guarantee that they will all be active when you are reading this book.

Library of Congress
Cataloging-in-Publication Data

Gagne, Tammy.
  Immigration in the US / by Tammy Gagne.
     pages cm. — (My guide to US citizenship)
  Includes bibliographical references and index.
  ISBN 978-1-61228-446-0 (library bound)
  1. Emigration and immigration law—United States—Juvenile literature. 2. Emigration and immigration—United States—Juvenile literature.
  I. Title. II. Title: Immigration in the United States.
  KF4819.85.G34 2013
  343.7308'2—dc23
                                                  2013023007

eBook ISBN: 9781612285061

                                                  PLB

CONTENTS

Words in **bold** appear in the Glossary.

More than four million people sailed to the United States from Ireland between 1820 and 1920. When these Irish immigrants arrived in the United States at Ellis Island, they had no idea what to expect in this new land. Some had family members who had already made the voyage, but others did not.

The Beginning of Immigration in the US

It had been a long journey for both mother and child. They had spent the last few months on a crowded ship bound for a place called New York. Finola and five-year-old Robert had traveled all the way from a little Irish town called Dunleer. Generations of O'Brennans had called Dunleer home, but a shortage of food had made it impossible for Finola and her husband William to survive in the rural community any longer.

William had been the first to make the journey to New York nearly two years earlier. When he arrived, he began looking for work and a place to live. He then saved as much money as he could so he could send for his wife and son. They missed each other terribly. At times they wondered if this day would ever come, but now it was finally

5

here. All three of them were ready to make a new home together in the United States of America.

More than sixty million Europeans have moved away from their home continent since the late 1400s.[1] Most of these people settled in the area that is now the United States. In addition to these travelers, Africans, Asians, and Latin Americans have also moved to the United States in large numbers. The reasons for their travels have been as different as the people themselves. When we study migration, though, we discover some common themes.

Leaving home to start a new life in a completely different place is a huge undertaking. In general, there are two types of reasons to make such a life-changing move. These are called *push* and *pull*. The word push refers to factors in a person's homeland that would make that person want to leave—they basically push the person to **emigrate**. These factors are usually extremely difficult circumstances such as flooding, war, or a lack of food. The word pull refers to factors in a new area that would make a person want to move there. A better climate, more available food, and the right to vote for leaders all pull people to new areas. Many times both push and pull affect a person's decision to move to a new land.

One of the most common reasons that people have **immigrated** to the United States over the last several centuries is money. If a person cannot earn enough money to survive in one place, they are forced to find work elsewhere. People have also come to the United States to get a better education. Some areas of the world offer fewer learning opportunities. By going to school in the United States, many people can get better jobs and make more money. Some of them choose to return to their homelands after they graduate, and some decide to stay in this country.

Religious freedom has brought many people to the United States as well. Whereas many countries have national

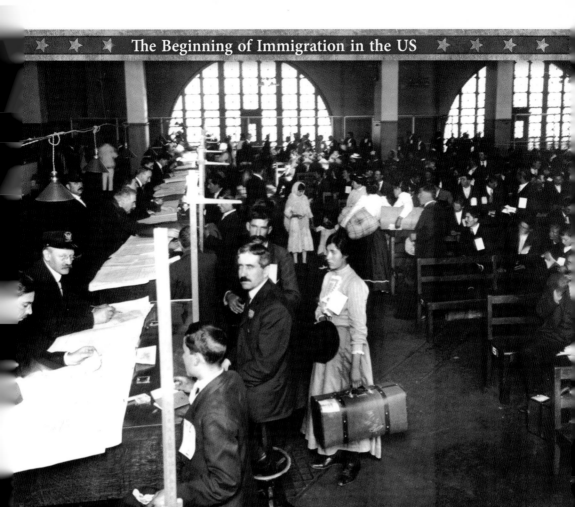

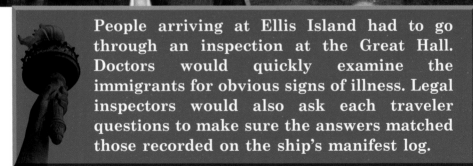

People arriving at Ellis Island had to go through an inspection at the Great Hall. Doctors would quickly examine the immigrants for obvious signs of illness. Legal inspectors would also ask each traveler questions to make sure the answers matched those recorded on the ship's manifest log.

religions, the United States does not require its citizens to practice a specific religion. The United States welcomes people of all faiths. It even welcomes those who practice no religion at all. In this way, our country is different from many other nations in the world.

The British colonies attracted about six hundred thousand European settlers to North America. In addition to these immigrants, the colonies also became home to about three hundred thousand African immigrants, most of them slaves.[2] While these numbers may sound like a lot, they represent only 2 percent of all the people who have immigrated to the United States over the course of history.

Following the American Revolution, several ethnic groups began immigrating to the United States in large numbers. These included Germans, Irish, French, Austro-Hungarians, and Scandinavians. From the 1830s to the 1880s, Germans made up more than one-quarter of all immigrants to the United States.[3] Most of these immigrants came to the United States for **economic** reasons. Their situations had much more to do with pull than push, however. No terrible disaster, financial or natural, caused them to leave their native land. Instead, they wanted to create better lives for themselves in a nation full of opportunities.

The German states officially came together to form a single nation in 1871. But even before this time, the **Industrial Revolution** was changing everyday life in Germany. German factories were attracting large numbers of people who used to make their livings as farmers. Being a farmer was becoming more and more difficult during this age. The best opportunities were in the cities. For these reasons, some young German men decided to move to the cities instead of taking over their families' farms.

Moving from a rural German state to an urban area was like starting a whole new life. Ultimately, many young Germans decided that making the longer trip across the Atlantic Ocean was worth the effort. Once in the United States, less than half of these German immigrants stayed in the cities.[4] The majority decided to settle in rural areas to make their livings as their fathers had—by living off the land.

In fact by 1870, more than one-third of all foreign-born farmers in the United States were German.[5]

Although many Germans came to the United States in the mid-1800s, even more Irish immigrants arrived here during the same time. From 1820 to 1860, Irish travelers made up

Manhattan's Little Italy neighborhood on Mulberry Street was created when Italian immigrants moved to New York. By 1900, immigrant families made up about 76 percent of New York City's population.

more than one-third of all immigrants to the United States.[6] The Irish people moved for very different reasons than the Germans did, however. Unlike Germany, Ireland was far from the forefront of the Industrial Revolution. While the rest of Europe seemed to be moving forward, Ireland was experiencing some major setbacks. The biggest of these was a severe food shortage known as the Irish Potato Famine, or simply the Great Famine. This difficulty was the greatest push for all Irish emigrants.

Some Irish immigrants became farmers in the United States, where food was easier to grow. The majority of Irish settlers moved to the cities, though. The mid-1800s was a time of great growth for most American cities. Buildings and roads were being built quickly, and small governments were developing to manage these areas. Irish immigrants were among the first workers to lay trolley tracks, and later they became the first trolley drivers. Irish immigrants and their children also made up a large percentage of the first policemen and firemen.

Scandinavian immigrants came to the United States from Denmark, Norway, and Sweden. Compared to the large numbers of German and Irish immigrants, this group was small. In comparison to the populations of these countries, though, the numbers were considerable. For a country as small as Norway, for example, losing 176,000 of its citizens in the 1880s meant a decrease in population of more than 9 percent.[7]

Swedish immigrants made up more than half of the 2.15 million immigrants from Scandinavia from 1820 to 1920.[8] Most of the Swedes came to the United States because their home country was becoming overpopulated—and land was harder and harder to get. Norwegians, on the other hand, had plenty of land, but only a small part of it could be farmed. Of the three Scandinavian countries, Denmark

During the early 1900s, both adults and children worked to help support their families. This Polish immigrant, known as Mrs. Bissie, and her children worked in the fields of both Baltimore, Maryland, and Biloxi, Mississippi.

contributed the smallest number of immigrants to the United States.

In addition to these immigrants, people came to the United States from the Mediterranean, Eastern Europe, and Asia at the end of the nineteenth century. Some also came from Cuba, Canada, Mexico, and South America. But non-

European travelers made up only a small percentage of the immigrants entering the United States at that time.

Back in 1808, the US government bought a tiny island in Upper New York Bay. The 3.5-acre land mass was purchased from the heirs of a local merchant named Samuel Ellis for $10,000. For decades, the property was used as a storage facility. But in 1890, the United States decided to build America's first federal immigration station on the site. The station became known as Ellis Island.[9]

But before immigration buildings were constructed on the island, the island was actually made bigger. Old subway tunnels from New York City and other large pieces of rubble were used as landfill. By the time the site was ready for construction, the island had doubled in size.

The Ellis Island Immigration Station opened its doors on January 1, 1892. On the first day of operation, seven hundred immigrants passed through Ellis Island. The island greeted nearly 450,000 immigrants during the first year alone.[10]

The first immigrant to pass through the Ellis Island Immigration Station on New Year's Day in 1892 was a fifteen-year-old girl named Annie Moore. She was from County Cork in Ireland. Annie and her two younger brothers had come to the United States to join their parents in New York City.

Five years later, a fire destroyed the original Ellis Island immigration station. It had been built from Georgia pine. Not only was the building lost in the blaze, but immigration records were lost as well. The Barge Office in Manhattan processed new immigrants until a new station was finally completed on Ellis Island three years later. This red brick structure with limestone trim still stands to this day. Although the Ellis Island Immigration Station no longer serves immigrants, the facility has been turned into a museum for the public.

Like Ellis Island, Angel Island in San Francisco Bay was the site of a United States immigration station in the early twentieth century. Unlike its sister station on the east coast, however, Angel Island was not always welcoming. Many immigrants were detained on this island for days, months, and in some cases even years while they awaited entry into the country.

The Chinese Exclusion Act of 1882 kept Chinese laborers from immigrating to the United States for sixty-one years. During this time it was very unusual to see women or children in the San Francisco area known as Chinatown. Known as a "bachelor society," it was made up almost entirely of men.

The Passing of Immigration Laws

Before reaching Ellis Island, boats carrying immigrants passed another small island called Liberty Island. This island is home to the Statue of Liberty, which greeted millions of passing immigrants in the late nineteenth and early twentieth centuries. A plaque on the statue reads "Give me your tired, your poor, your huddled masses yearning to breathe free."[1] The founders of the United States felt that it was important to welcome immigrants to their country. But even before the Statue of Liberty was constructed, the United States had begun to create laws to make it more difficult to enter the country. There were even laws to keep out all people from certain countries.

When the United States was first formed, any free white person who

15

had lived in the country for at least two years could apply to become a US citizen. But in 1798, the Alien and Sedition Acts were passed. These new laws required a person to live in the United States for fourteen years before applying for citizenship. The president could also **deport** foreigners that he judged "dangerous to the peace and safety of the United States."[2] And if the United States went to war with another country, immigrants from that country could now be imprisoned or deported.

Nearly a century after the Alien and Sedition Acts were passed, immigration continued to be a source of great political debate. The government was also changing how it viewed immigrants from different parts of the world.

As many as three hundred thousand Chinese immigrants arrived in the United States between 1848 and 1882.[3] This time period was one of great poverty in China. The United States, however, was in the midst of the California Gold Rush. Unlike the European immigrants, the Chinese entered the country on the west coast, most in San Francisco. They then settled in the surrounding areas, working as farmers, miners, and servants. As many as ten thousand Chinese people helped to build the western leg of the Central Pacific Railroad.[4]

The biggest difference between Chinese immigrants and those from other lands was the way they were treated by both the American people and government. Many American workers disliked Chinese immigrants because they were willing to work for so little money. Even very low wages in America were higher than what the Chinese people could earn at home. The Americans feared that if the Chinese were willing to do the same jobs for less money, there would be no jobs left for them. The government was also concerned that too many Chinese people were coming into the country.

Congress passed the Chinese Exclusion Act in 1882. It was signed into law by President Chester A. Arthur. This law denied

Chinese workers were willing to work very hard for extremely low pay during the late 1800s. Chinese laborers transported enough dirt to fill in the Secret Town Trestle, shown here, in the Sierra Nevada Mountain range.

Chinese people already in the United States the right to become US citizens. Furthermore, it denied immigration to Chinese laborers for the next decade. At the end of this ten-year period, the law was renewed as the Geary Act. It was then made permanent in 1902. The laws were changed in 1917 to exclude almost anyone from Asia.

The Emergency Quota Act of 1921 became law during the presidency of Warren Harding. It created **quotas** to control immigration. Each country was allowed only a certain number of immigrants each year. These pre-set limits favored immigrants from northern

HIP! HURRAH!
CHINESE EXCLUDED
The
Democratic Chinese- Exclusion Bill
Has Been Signed by
OUR DEMOCRATIC PRESIDENT
Hip! Hurrah! The White Man is on Top.
Let every DEMOCRAT and all other GOOD Cit-
izens turn out and Ratify this
DEMOCRATIC MEASURE
At the
HORTON HOUSE PLAZA
This Wednesday Evening at 8 O'clock.
To-Night
Speeches will be made by Leading Demo-
cratic Orators.
COME OUT AND RATIFY:
Come Everybody!
NO MORE CHINESE!
By Order of
Democratic County Central Committee,

Congress of the United States, *At the First Session,*

Begun and held at the CITY OF WASHINGTON, in the DISTRICT OF COLUMBIA, on Monday, the *fifth* day of *December*, eighteen hundred and eighty- *one*

An Act

To execute certain treaty stipulations relating to Chinese.

Whereas, In the opinion of the Government of the United States the coming of Chinese laborers to this country endangers the good order of certain localities within the territory thereof: Therefore, **Be it enacted by the Senate and House of Representatives of the United States of America in Congress assembled,** That from and after the expiration of ninety days next after the passage of this act, and until the expiration of ten years next after the passage of this act, the coming of Chinese laborers to the United States be, and the same is hereby, suspended; and during such suspension it shall not be lawful for any Chinese laborer to come, or, having so come after the expiration of said ninety days, to remain within the United States.

SEC. 2. That the master of any vessel who shall knowingly bring within the United States on such vessel, and land or permit to be landed, any Chinese laborer, from any foreign port or place, shall be deemed guilty of a misdemeanor, and on conviction thereof shall be punished by a fine of not more than five hundred dollars for each and every such Chinese laborer so brought, and may be also imprisoned for a term not exceeding one year.

SEC. 3. That the two foregoing sections shall not apply to Chinese laborers who were in the United States on the seventeenth day of November, eighteen hundred and eighty, or who shall have come into the same before the expiration of ninety days next after the passage of this act, and who shall produce

THE ONLY ONE BARRED OUT.
ENLIGHTENED AMERICAN STATESMAN.—" We must draw the line *somewhere*, you know."

This 1882 political cartoon depicts the new immigration laws that singled out the Chinese. The text reads, "The only one barred out. Enlightened American Statesman—'We must draw the line somewhere, you know.'"

and western Europe, however. Only small numbers of people from southern and western Europe were allowed to enter the country, and Asians were still denied entry completely. The bans on Chinese immigration and naturalization continued until 1943 when all exclusion laws were finally reversed.

But this reversal didn't change much. Congress began using quotas as a means of controlling Chinese immigration instead. The United States allowed a total of 105 Chinese immigrants to enter the United States in 1943.[5] The negative attitude towards Asian immigrants would eventually change over the next two decades.

Ultimately, Congress passed the Immigration Act of 1965. This act was signed into law by President Lyndon B. Johnson. It loosened many of the restrictions on US immigration. Under this new law, up to 170,000 immigrants from the Eastern Hemisphere could enter the country each year. No more than twenty thousand of these could be from any one country, however. The people who would be allowed into

During the nineteenth century, male immigrants entering the United States outnumbered females by a large margin. This was true of travelers from all over the world, but it was most noticeable among Chinese immigrants. For every Chinese woman who immigrated to the United States, twenty Chinese men entered the country.[6]

Seated at the foot of the Statue of Liberty, President Lyndon B. Johnson signed the Immigration Act of 1965 into law. The bill abolished the National Origins Formula that had been in place in the United States since the Emergency Quota Act.

the country would be chosen based on three factors: skills, the need for **political asylum**, and family ties in the United States.

No major changes were made to the immigration system until Congress passed the Immigration Act of 1990. Signed into law by President George Bush, this law loosened restrictions even further. **Visas** would now be issued for more reasons. They included the creation of new businesses and the increase of ethnic diversity. It also stated that no one country could receive more than 7 percent of the total visas issued.

The Chinese Telephone Exchange served San Francisco's Chinatown area from 1887 until 1949. In Chinese culture, it was rude to refer to people by numbers. For this reason, the operators memorized the name, number, and address of every subscriber.

How Do Immigrants Affect the US Economy?

Many things about immigration have changed since the nineteenth century, but one remains very much the same: many Americans still worry that immigrants make it harder for current United States citizens to earn a living. Like the Chinese immigrants of the mid-1900s, today's Mexican immigrants are known for working for less money than other US residents. Some citizens believe that the immigrants' willingness to work for so little drives down wages for American citizens as well.

Certainly, it is true that more people can mean greater competition for jobs. This is not the only effect that a higher population has on jobs, however. When the number of people increases, the need for goods and services also increases. Every single person in the United States needs food, clothing, shelter, and transportation. More people means that farmers will have to grow more crops, manufacturers will have to produce more clothing, builders will have to construct more houses and stores, and carmakers will have to produce more vehicles. As more people fill these jobs, the government is able to collect more taxes. This allows the government to hire more teachers to fill the growing need for education. Tax money also helps create jobs through work such as road repairs.

With this in mind, you may wonder why the unemployment rate is so high when the population of the country is higher than it has ever been. While it is easy to blame immigrants for taking all the jobs, there are many other reasons that jobs have become harder to come by in recent years. One reason is that many companies have moved their production plants outside of the United States to save money. Mexico is actually one of the countries to which many US businesses have moved factories in recent years. Ford, General Electric, General Motors, and RCA are just a few of the big American names who have moved assembly plants to Mexico. General Electric alone employs thirty thousand people in thirty-five different factories in Mexico.[1]

An auto worker helps assemble a Ford Fiesta at this Ford factory in Cuautitlan Izcalli, Mexico. Ford is one of the many American companies that have moved their factories outside the US in recent years.

According to a new report by the Banco Bilbao Vizcaya Argentaria (BBVA), Mexican immigrants were responsible for between 3.7 and 4.1 percent of the gross domestic product (GDP) of the United States between 2003 and 2011. The report issued by the multinational Spanish banking group showed that their biggest contribution to the GDP is in agriculture, despite the fact that less than 5 percent of Mexican immigrants work in farming.

Contribution to GDP of Mexican Immigrants, by Economic Sectors (percent contribution of sectoral GDP)

Industry	2003	2004	2005	2006	2007	2008	2009	2010	2011p
Agriculture, forestry, and fishing	17.3	18.9	21.9	19.0	18.5	16.9	17.8	18.9	16.3
Construction	10.0	12.2	13.6	14.2	15.7	14.3	12.1	12.7	13.4
Accommodation and food services	10.2	10.1	10.3	11.1	11.0	10.7	11.2	11.5	9.9
Nondurable goods manufacturing	6.5	7.1	6.0	6.7	7.2	6.5	7.6	7.6	7.4
Wholesale trade	5.4	5.2	5.0	3.9	5.0	5.6	5.1	5.6	6.0
Other services, except government	5.5	6.0	6.1	5.3	6.4	6.1	6.0	6.3	5.8
Durable goods manufacturing	5.2	4.5	5.0	5.4	5.5	5.4	5.3	5.1	5.1
Professional and business services	3.0	3.7	3.6	3.3	3.4	3.5	3.4	4.0	4.2
Transportation and warehousing	3.5	3.3	3.1	3.7	4.1	4.0	4.0	4.6	4.1
Retail trade	3.4	3.8	3.5	3.6	3.9	3.8	3.5	3.9	3.8
Mining, oil and gas extration	6.2	7.2	3.8	4.7	3.3	4.0	1.6	4.3	3.7
Educational services, health care, and social assistance	1.5	1.4	1.5	1.5	1.5	1.7	1.7	2.0	1.9
Arts, entertainment, and recreation	2.3	2.4	2.0	3.4	2.9	1.9	2.0	2.3	1.9
Finances, insurance, real estate, and leasing	2.5	2.1	2.2	2.6	2.2	2.0	2.0	1.5	1.7
Utilities	2.3	0.7	1.6	1.4	1.6	1.2	1.1	1.8	1.6
Information Services	1.5	1.1	1.6	1.1	1.2	1.4	1.7	2.0	1.5
Government	0.9	0.7	0.6	0.9	1.1	0.9	1.0	1.1	1.1
National	3.8	3.8	3.9	4.0	4.1	3.9	3.7	3.8	3.8

Note: The seventeen branches of the Table are calculated by adding the contributions to GDP of the fifty-four sectors in which data on employment and average productivity in the US are broken down.
p = Preliminary data.
Source: BBVA Research with data from the CPS March supplement and the Bureau of Economic Analysis, 2003–2011.

The US-born children of both legal and illegal immigrants are legal citizens of the United States. These first-generation Americans have all the same rights as any other citizen of the country.

As of January 2013, the unemployment rate in the United States was 7.9 percent.[2] Although the number of people out of work is undeniably high, consider an even harder time in our history before linking the lack of jobs to the population of immigrants. Just before the Great Depression, the government had enacted several laws which limited immigration. During the depression, immigration rates dropped even lower, but the unemployment rate in the United States was over 20 percent.

Many Americans also worry that immigrants are a burden to our tax system. These citizens might assume that immigrants don't pay taxes, but this isn't true. Every immigrant who is in the United States legally pays the same taxes as any other resident. Both legal and **illegal immigrants** pay sales taxes, restaurant taxes, gasoline taxes, and property taxes. Even immigrants who don't own their own cars or homes pay into the tax system when they ride a bus or rent an apartment. The owners of these businesses pay taxes on the money they charge their customers, whether they are immigrants or not.

Illegal immigrants often work under the table. This means that their employers pay them in cash and don't report them as employees to the government. No income taxes, Social Security taxes, or Medicare taxes are paid by these workers. Frequently, these jobs come from individuals or families who need help with things like caring for their children, cleaning, or gardening. Most companies, though, won't provide work to a person who doesn't have a **social security number**. Some illegal immigrants use fake social security numbers to get jobs. These immigrants actually pay taxes without receiving any of the benefits that our government provides.

It is estimated that illegal immigrants actually pay about $7 billion in taxes each year this way.[3]

Many Americans also worry that immigrants take advantage of public service programs. Immigrants with children, for instance, send their kids to public schools. Immigrants also use emergency medical care as well as the services of police and fire departments when necessary. Some immigrants can also use certain welfare programs, such as food stamps and free or reduced-cost school breakfasts and lunches for their children.

But others would argue that helping immigrant families actually helps make our economy stronger. When immigrants are given the chance to remain in the United States legally, they are able to get better educations and higher-paying jobs. This in turn reduces the need for welfare benefits.

There are two main types of visas issued by the US government. People who visit the United States for vacation, students who are part of foreign exchange programs, and those who come to the United States to work for a short period of time are given nonimmigrant visas. People who come to the United States with plans to live in the country long term are given immigrant visas. Both types of visas have expiration dates.

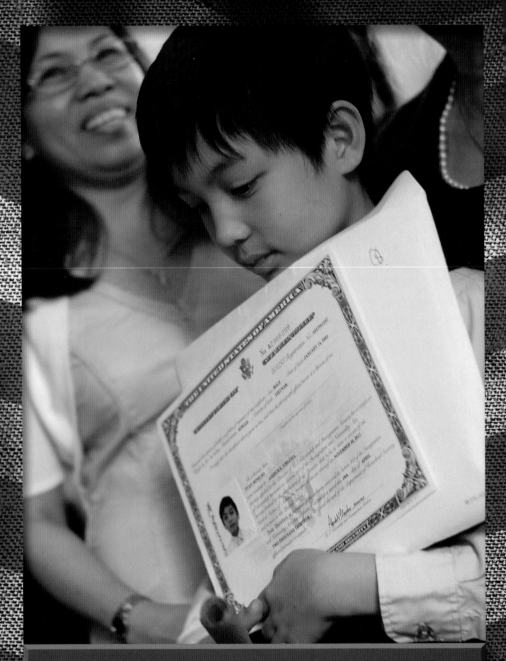

Children who immigrate to the United States automatically gain citizenship when their parents become citizens. On April 29, 2013, twenty children participated in a special ceremony to celebrate their new citizenship. The children, including Tuan Minh Do, shown here, took the Oath of Allegiance in the Emancipation Room of President Lincoln's Cottage.

The Language of US Immigration

It has been a long time since Europeans represented the largest number of immigrants to the United States. By 2004, only 16 percent of US immigrants were coming from Europe and Canada combined. The largest group—31 percent—was coming from Mexico. And another 26 percent were traveling to the United States from Asia.[1] Still, the cultures of Britain and other European countries continue to influence the culture of the United States in many ways. Language is one of Britain's most obvious impacts on our country.

Even though the United States doesn't have an official language, English is spoken in most schools, businesses, and other public places. Immigrants are expected to learn the language and be able to speak it in these settings. When a person cannot speak English well, it makes it difficult for him or her to interview for jobs. It can also make it harder to perform a job well once he or she has been hired. Learning English is a requirement for becoming a **naturalized** citizen.

Children coming to the United States usually have an easier time learning English than their parents and grandparents. Even when their native language is spoken at home, kids speak English on a daily basis with their friends and teachers in the classroom. But adult immigrants need to learn English, too.

Congress passed the Immigration Reform and Control Act in 1986. It was signed into law by President Ronald Reagan. This new set of laws provided many illegal immigrants with the opportunity to become citizens. Those who wished to go through the naturalization process still had to meet certain requirements, however. In addition to learning about United States history and government, these immigrants also had to learn English.

Today, more and more immigrants are finding it difficult to accomplish this goal. A study by a New York City organization examined the problem. The study revealed that the number of immigrants living on Long Island who don't speak English increased by 12 percent between 2005 and 2009. During this same time period, the number of immigrants attending publicly funded language classes decreased by 25 percent.[2]

Tom Hilliard, the author of the study, insists that the reason isn't lack of interest. He believes that there simply aren't enough classes out there. He says it is important for the state of New York to create more learning opportunities for this growing part of the population. "Immigrants are a tremendously important economic engine, but lack of English proficiency holds them back from realizing their full potential as workers, as business owners, and as citizens."[3]

Not speaking English can make nearly every part of everyday life difficult for immigrants. People who don't know English cannot ask for directions if they become lost. If they become sick, they cannot get the medical care they need without the help of an interpreter. Even helping their children with their homework becomes a challenge for these immigrants.

Many Americans also disagree about whether United States citizenship should be a birthright. The Birthright Citizenship Act of 2011 would have reversed this right that was granted by the Fourteenth Amendment to the US Constitution. The bill proposed to only offer citizenship to children born in the United States if one parent was a citizen, permanent resident, or serving in the US Military. The House Judiciary Committee decided not to enact the law.

Education has been shown to play a key role in how well many immigrants speak English. Sixty-two percent of Hispanic immigrants with college degrees speak English very well. For those with high school diplomas only, the percentage drops to 34 percent. It falls even lower for those who have not finished high school—all the way down to 11 percent.[4]

One hundred fifty immigrants from thirty-eight different countries became US citizens on May 17, 2013, at the US Citizenship and Immigration Services (USCIS) in New York City. The soon-to-be naturalized citizens stood as they listened to the national anthem being played as part of the ceremony.

Certain lawmakers have been trying to make English the official language of the United States for years. Congressman Steve King of Iowa is one of them. He states, "A common language is the most powerful unifying force known throughout history. We need to encourage **assimilation** of all legal immigrants in each generation. A nation divided by language cannot pull together as effectively as a people."[5]

Senator James Inhofe of Oklahoma agrees. "Speaking English is a guaranteed way for new immigrants to succeed in school, increase their earning potential, and enhance their career options." He adds, "This nation decided long ago that you must know English to become a citizen. So there is no reason to offer government services in foreign languages. In the same way that the Pledge of Allegiance and the National Anthem bring this nation together, English is something we share and should promote."[6]

Not everyone supports the idea of making English—or any other language—the single, official language of the United States. The American Civil Liberties Union (ACLU) opposes the idea strongly. As the ACLU explains on its website, "The problem is not that immigrants are unwilling to learn English, but that there are not enough available educational resources for them. Today, many thousands of immigrants throughout the country are on the waiting lists for adult English classes. English-only laws do nothing constructive to increase English proficiency, they simply discriminate against and punish those who have not yet learned English."[7]

For the last four decades, Hispanics represented the largest number of new US immigrants. By 2010, however, 36 percent of new immigrants were Asian. Hispanics made up only 31 percent of new arrivals into the country that year.[8]

California's Proposition 187 was met by many demonstrations in 1994. Still, it passed in November of that year. The purpose of the law was to require police, health care providers, and teachers to report the immigration status of all individuals. The law was voided in 1999.

Is That Constitutional?

In addition to federal laws, some states have also passed their own laws relating to immigration. The United States Constitution allows each state to make many of its own laws. The amount of sales tax people pay in one state, for example, may be much higher than the amount people pay in another. Some states have no sales tax at all. When it comes to the subject of immigration, however, many people disagree about how much power the states should have on their own.

Should the states be able to override decisions made by the federal government? Throughout our history, states have used the law to deny rights to certain groups of people. When the Fifteenth Amendment granted African Americans the right to vote in 1870, many southern states did everything in their power to stop this change from happening. They decided to start giving literacy tests and charging poll taxes to keep newly freed slaves from voting. They knew that most African Americans couldn't read. They also knew that it would be hard for them to come up with the money for this new tax. Eventually both of these barriers to voting were outlawed by the federal government, but it took many years.

Over the last century, many states have continued to find ways to bypass federal laws. Some states have even created their own laws to control immigration. In 1994, California passed Proposition 187. This law required health care providers, police, and teachers to tell the government when they encountered illegal immigrants. Its supporters wanted to make sure that illegal immigrants would not benefit from services provided with tax money. "Prop 187," as it became known, angered many people. Just days after the law passed, a federal district court judge insisted that it violated the US Constitution. An **injunction** was put in place to keep the law from going into effect until a federal court could look more closely at the matter.

Nearly three years after Proposition 187 passed, US District Judge Mariana Pfaelzer ruled that the measure was unconstitutional. California's Assembly Speaker Antonio Villaraigosa had this to say about the reversal: "The decision ensures that children can get an education, working families can get health care, and law enforcement can focus on

Many people forget that slaves were also immigrants. The biggest difference between the slaves and other immigrants was that the slaves didn't come to this country willingly. It took much longer for slaves to be granted the status of United States citizens than most other immigrants.

fighting crime. We stand together today to say in one loud voice that Californians are tired of wedge issues and culture wars."[1]

Although this battle was over, the war over immigration would continue. As the United States has entered the twenty-first century, many Americans still think that the federal government isn't doing enough to control immigration. In 2010, the state of Arizona passed SB 1070. This state law granted police the right to stop any person they suspect of being an illegal immigrant. This meant that immigrants would have to carry their immigration paperwork at all times. It also meant that people could be stopped by the police just for looking like an immigrant.

People from all over the country began voicing their opinions about Arizona's new law. Many of them felt that SB 1070, like California's Proposition 187, was unconstitutional. Some of them even issued **boycotts** of Arizona companies and their products. Other Americans insisted that SB 1070 was simply about enforcing laws already on the books. The issue went before the US Supreme Court in 2012. The court decided that police could indeed ask for a person's immigration paperwork, but only during a legal stop when the officer has a reasonable suspicion.

This decision did little to settle disagreements among the people. Omar Jadwat is a lawyer who works with the American Civil Liberties Union's Immigrants' Rights Project. He says, "Law enforcement resources are wasted when people are targeted based on their skin color, and our core American values of fairness and equality are compromised. The ACLU will continue to fight against SB 1070."[2]

Arizona Governor Jan Brewer has a different opinion. "I've never claimed that SB 1070 would cure Arizona's problems with illegal immigration; only the federal government has the resources and responsibility necessary to achieve that. What SB 1070 does represent is one more tool that our officers can

In rallies like this one in downtown Los Angeles on May 1, 2010, immigrant rights activists let the world know how unfair they thought Arizona's SB 1070 was. The US Supreme Court decided that the police could indeed ask for an immigrant's paperwork, but only during a legal stop with reasonable suspicion.

use in collaborating with federal authorities to reduce the crime and other impacts associated with illegal immigration in our communities."

Brewer goes on to say, "It is not enough that SB 1070 be enforced. It must be enforced efficiently, effectively, and in harmony with the Constitution and **civil rights**. I have full faith and confidence that Arizona's state and local law enforcement officers are prepared for this task."[3]

Disagreements about immigration in the United States are sure to continue for the foreseeable future. The laws in Arizona and California are just two examples of immigration legislation at the state level. More than two hundred immigration laws were passed in forty states between 2007 and 2009 alone.[4] Many of these laws and many new laws that follow will almost certainly make their way to the US Supreme Court.

Some immigrants who become United States citizens possess dual citizenship. This means that they are citizens of two countries at the same time. Not all countries allow dual citizenship. Immigrants from countries that don't allow dual citizenship must choose between remaining a citizen of their home country and becoming a naturalized US citizen.

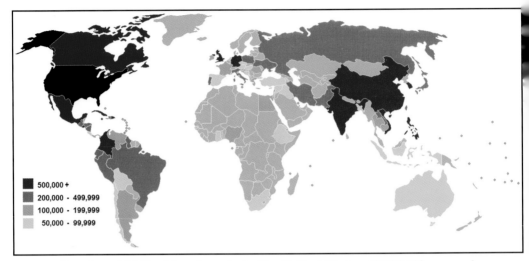

Country of birth of immigrants in the United States (2000 US census)

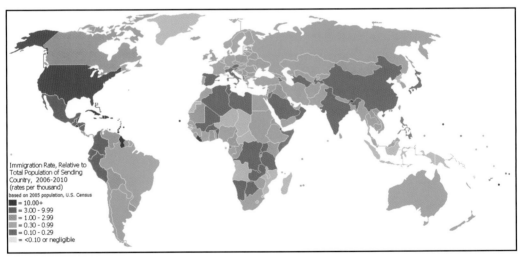

This graphic shows which countries sent the most immigrants to the United States, in relation to their total population. The numbers on the left represent the number of legal immigrants to the US from 2006 to 2010, for every 2,000 people in the home country.

Late 1400s	Europeans begin traveling to North America.
1607	Jamestown, the first British settlement in America, is established in the colony of Virginia.
1700–1800	The peak of the Atlantic slave trade; over six million slaves are brought from Africa to the Americas during this time.
1750–1850	The Industrial Revolution changes the way goods are manufactured throughout the world.
1775–1783	The American Revolutionary War is fought, resulting in the United States of America becoming an independent nation.
1798	President John Adams signs the Alien and Sedition Acts into law.
1807	Britain outlaws the slave trade.
1808	The United States buys a small island in Upper New York Bay that becomes known as Ellis Island.
1845–1851	The Irish Potato Famine.
1865	The Thirteenth Amendment abolishes slavery.
1868	The Fourteenth Amendment establishes birthright citizenship in the United States.
1870	The Fifteenth Amendment gives African American men the right to vote.
1871	The German states unite to become the nation of Germany.
1882	President Chester A. Arthur signs the Chinese Exclusion Act into law.
1890	The United States begins construction on the Ellis Island Immigration Station.
1892	The Ellis Island Immigration Station opens; Congress passes the Geary Act.
1897	Fire destroys the original Ellis Island Immigration Station.
1900	The Ellis Island Immigration Station reopens.
1902	Congress makes the Chinese Exclusion Act permanent.
1921	President Warren Harding signs the Emergency Quota Act into law.
1930s	The Great Depression.
1943	All of the Exclusion Acts are reversed.
1965	President Lyndon B. Johnson signs the Immigration Act of 1965 into law.
1986	Ronald Reagan signs the Immigration Reform and Control Act into law.
1990	President George Bush signs the Immigration Act of 1990 into law.
1994	The state of California passes Proposition 187.
1997	US District Judge Mariana Pfaelzer rules that Proposition 187 is unconstitutional.
2004	Thirty-one percent of all US immigrants come from Mexico.
2007–2009	More than two hundred immigration laws are passed in forty different states.
2010	Asians surpass Hispanics as the largest immigrant group in the United States; the state of Arizona passes SB 1070.
2012	The Supreme Court upholds the part of SB 1070 that enables police officers to ask for a person's immigration paperwork, but only during a legal stop when the officer has a reasonable suspicion.
2013	With a vote of 68-32, the US Senate passes a major immigration reform bill. The move is the biggest step toward immigration overhaul since 1986.

Chapter 1

1. Roger Daniels, *Coming to America: A History of Immigration and Ethnicity in American Life* (New York: Perennial, 2002), p. 11.
2. Ibid., p. 30.
3. Ibid., p. 145.
4. Ibid., p. 149.
5. Ibid., p. 151.
6. Ibid., p. 127.
7. Ibid., p. 164.
8. Ibid.
9. The Statue of Liberty-Ellis Island Foundation, Inc., "Ellis Island—Timeline." http://www.ellisisland.org/genealogy/ellis_island_timeline.asp
10. Ibid.

Chapter 2

1. National Park Service, Statue of Liberty Photo Gallery, "The New Colossus." http://www.nps.gov/stli/images/20060817112944.gif
2. Ourdocuments.gov, "Transcript of Alien and Sedition Acts (1798)." http://www.ourdocuments.gov/doc.php?flash=true&doc=16&page=transcript
3. Roger Daniels, *Coming to America: A History of Immigration and Ethnicity in American Life* (New York: Perennial, 2002), p. 239.
4. Ibid., p. 243.
5. Angel Island Immigration Station Foundation, "Chinese Immigration in the 19th and Early 20th Centuries." http://www.ourdocuments.gov/doc.php?doc=47
6. Roger Daniels, *Coming to America: A History of Immigration and Ethnicity in American Life* (New York: Perennial, 2002), p. 241.

Chapter 3

1. Dustin Ensinger, *Economy in Crisis: America's Economic Report*, "Whirlpool Moving Jobs to Mexico," February 22, 2010. http://economyincrisis.org/content/whirlpool-moving-jobs-mexico
2. United States Department of Labor, Bureau of Labor Statistics, "The Employment Situation." http://www.bls.gov/news.release/pdf/empsit.pdf
3. Eduardo Porter, *The New York Times*, "Illegal Immigrants Are Bolstering Social Security with Billions," April 5, 2005.

Chapter 4

1. Grant Makers Concerned with Immigrants and Refugees (GMIR), "US Immigration Statistics." http://www.gcir.org/immigration/facts/statistics
2. Victor Manuel Ramos, *Newsday*, "English Classes for Immigrants Decline," January 19, 2012.
3. Ibid.
4. Shirin Hakimzadeh and D'Vera Cohn, "English Usage Among Hispanics in the United States," Pew Hispanic Center, November 29, 2007. http://www.pewhispanic.org/2007/11/29/english-usage-among-hispanics-in-the-united-states/
5. Brian Montopoli, "Bill Would Make English Official Language of US Government," CBS News, March 11, 2011. http://www.cbsnews.com/8301-503544_162-20042244-503544.html
6. James M. Inhofe and Cecilia Muñoz, *New York Times Upfront*, "Should English Be Declared America's National Language?" October 23, 2006.
7. American Civil Liberties Union, "The Rights of Immigrants-ACLU Position Paper," September 8, 2000. http://www.aclu.org/immigrants-rights/rights-immigrants-aclu-position-paper
8. Kirk Semple, *The New York Times*, "In a Shift, Biggest Wave of Migrants Is Now Asian," June 18, 2012. http://www.nytimes.com/2012/06/19/us/asians-surpass-hispanics-as-biggest-immigrant-wave.html?_r=0

Chapter 5

1. American Civil Liberties Union, "CA's Anti-Immigrant Proposition 187 is Voided, Ending State's Five-Year Battle with ACLU, Rights Groups," July 29, 1999. http://www.aclu.org/immigrants-rights/cas-anti-immigrant-proposition-187-voided-ending-states-five-year-battle-aclu-righ
2. Ted Hesson, "Can Arizona's SB 1070 and Civil Rights Coexist? Jan Brewer Thinks So," ABC News, September 18, 2012. http://abcnews.go.com/ABC_Univision/News/arizonas-sb-1070-civil-rights-coexist-jan-brewer/story?id=17266035
3. Ibid.
4. Daniel B. Wood, *The Christian Science Monitor*, "After Arizona, Why Are 10 States Considering Immigration Bills?" May 10, 2010. http://www.csmonitor.com/USA/Society/2010/0510/After-Arizona-why-are-10-states-considering-immigration-bills

Books

Challen, Paul. *Migration in the 21st Century*. New York: Crabtree Publishing, 2010.

Roza, Greg. *Immigration and Migration: The Story of America*. New York: Gareth Stevens Publishing, 2011.

Walker, Robert. *Pushes and Pulls*. New York: Crabtree Publishing, 2010.

On the Internet

National Geographic: "Xpeditions." http://www.nationalgeographic.com/xpeditions/lessons/09/g68/migrationguidestudent.pdf

The Statue of Liberty-Ellis Island Foundation, Inc.: "Ellis Island." http://www.ellisisland.org/genealogy/ellis_island.asp

U.S. History: Pre-Columbian to the New Millennium: "The Alien and Sedition Acts." http://www.ushistory.org/us/19e.asp

Works Consulted

American Civil Liberties Union. "CA's Anti-Immigrant Proposition 187 is Voided, Ending State's Five-Year Battle with ACLU, Rights Groups." July 29, 1999. http://www.aclu.org/immigrants-rights/cas-anti-immigrant-proposition-187-voided-ending-states-five-year-battle-aclu-righ

American Civil Liberties Union. "The Rights of Immigrants-ACLU Position Paper." September 8, 2000. http://www.aclu.org/immigrants-rights/rights-immigrants-aclu-position-paper

Angel Island Immigration Station Foundation. "Chinese Immigration in the 19th and Early 20th Centuries." http://www.ourdocuments.gov/doc.php?doc=47

Bausum, Ann. *Denied, Detained, Deported: Stories From the Dark Side of American Immigration*. Washington, DC: National Geographic, 2009.

Chomsky, Aviva. *"They Take Our Jobs!" And 20 Other Myths About Immigration*. Boston, Massachusetts: Beacon Press, 2007.

Daniels, Roger. *Coming to America: A History of Immigration and Ethnicity in American Life*. New York: Perennial, 2002.

Daniels, Roger. *Guarding the Golden Door*. New York: Hill and Wang, 2004.

Ensinger, Dustin. "Whirlpool Moving Jobs to Mexico." *Economy in Crisis: America's Economic Report*, February 22, 2010. http://economyincrisis.org/content/whirlpool-moving-jobs-mexico

Grant Makers Concerned with Immigrants and Refugees (GMIR). "US Immigration Statistics." http://www.gcir.org/immigration/facts/statistics

Hakimzadeh, Shirin, and D'Vera Cohn. "English Usage Among Hispanics in the United States." Pew Hispanic Center, November 29, 2007. http://www.pewhispanic.org/2007/11/29/english-usage-among-hispanics-in-the-united-states/

Hesson, Ted. "Can Arizona's SB 1070 and Civil Rights Coexist? Jan Brewer Thinks So." ABC News, September 18, 2012. http://abcnews.go.com/ABC_Univision/News/arizonas-sb-1070-civil-rights-coexist-jan-brewer/story?id=17266035

Inhofe, James M., and Cecilia Muñoz. "Should English Be Declared America's National Language?" *New York Times Upfront*, October 23, 2006.

Montopoli, Brian. "Bill Would Make English Official Language of US Government." CBS News, March 11, 2011. http://www.cbsnews.com/8301-503544_162-20042244-503544.html

National Park Service. "The New Colossus." *Statue of Liberty Photo Gallery*. http://www.nps.gov/stli/images/20060817112944.gif

Ourdocuments.gov. "Chinese Exclusion Act (1882)." http://www.ourdocuments.gov/doc.php?doc=47

Ourdocuments.gov. "Transcript of Alien and Sedition Acts (1798)." http://www.ourdocuments.gov/doc.php?flash=true&doc=16&page=transcript

Porter, Eduardo. "Illegal Immigrants Are Bolstering Social Security with Billions," *The New York Times*, April 5, 2005.

Ramos, Victor Manuel. "English Classes for Immigrants Decline." *Newsday*, January 19, 2012.

Semple, Kirk. "In a Shift, Biggest Wave of Migrants Is Now Asian." *The New York Times*, June 18, 2012. http://www.nytimes.com/2012/06/19/us/asians-surpass-hispanics-as-biggest-immigrant-wave.html?_r=0

The Statue of Liberty-Ellis Island Foundation, Inc., "Ellis Island—Timeline." http://www.ellisisland.org/genealogy/ellis_island_timeline.asp

Swain, Carol M., Editor. *Debating Immigration*. New York: Cambridge University Press, 2007.

United States Department of Labor, Bureau of Labor Statistics. "The Employment Situation." February 1, 2013. http://www.bls.gov/news.release/pdf/empsit.pdf

Wood, Daniel B. "After Arizona, Why Are 10 States Considering Immigration Bills?" *The Christian Science Monitor*, May 10, 2010. http://www.csmonitor.com/USA/Society/2010/0510/After-Arizona-why-are-10-states-considering-immigration-bills

assimilation (uh-sim-uh-LEY-shuhn)—The act of becoming part of another culture.

boycott (BOI-kot)—To abstain from buying or using a group or business's products, usually an attempt to force that group or business to change their practices.

civil rights (SIV-uhl RAHYTS)—The rights of the people in a free and equal society.

deport (dih-POHRT)—To forcibly remove from the country.

economic (ek-uh-NOM-ik)—Relating to the production and use of goods, services, money, and wealth.

emigrate (EM-i-greyt)—To leave one's country to settle in another.

illegal immigrant (ih-LEE-guhl IM-i-gruhnt)—A person who enters a country without the permission of the government.

immigrate (IM-i-greyt)—To enter a country with the intention of settling there.

Industrial Revolution (in-DUHS-tree-uhl rev-uh-LOO-shuhn)—The rapid development of machine-based businesses, roughly between 1750 and 1850.

injunction (in-JUHNGK-shuhn)—A judicial order to refrain from performing a particular act.

naturalize (NACH-er-uh-lahyz)—To grant national citizenship to an immigrant.

political asylum (puh-LIT-i-kuhl uh-SAHY-luhm)—Entry and protection offered by one nation to refugees from another nation where the government may endanger its citizens.

quota (KWOH-tuh)—A fixed number that is allowed in a certain time, as in immigrants allowed into the country.

social security number (SOH-shuhl si-KYOOR-i-tee)—A nine-digit number used by the US government to identify taxpayers.

visa (VEE-zuh)—Legal paperwork giving a person the right to stay in a country for a specific amount of time.

About the
AUTHOR

Tammy Gagne is the author of numerous books for adults and children, including *A Kid's Guide to the Voting Process* and *Life on the Reservations* for Mitchell Lane Publishers. She resides in northern New England with her husband and son. One of her favorite pastimes is visiting schools to speak to kids about the writing process.